THE LOGIC OF PROPERTY

SIMON MEEHAN

Published by Brolga Publishing Pty Ltd
ABN 46 063 962 443
PO Box 452
Torquay 3228 VIC
Australia

email: markzocchi@brolgapublishing.com.au

ISBN: 978-1-7640776-0-6

Printed in Australia

Cover design by Luke Harris, WorkingType Studio

Typeset by WorkingType Studio

Contents

Foreword

Simon and I grew up together, living only 7 doors down from one another, we went to primary school, played footy and everything else kids did together. Amazingly in 2004 when we both visited Ireland (ancestral home for Fitzgerald's and Meehan's) he was with me with a second cousin of mine in six mile bridge County Clare, looking at my great grandfathers grave when we realised his great grandfather was buried 3km away. It's an amazing life no doubt.

Simons special talent is his ability to motivate people to take action. This sounds simple but it's not easy as 99% of people procrastinate, especially when it comes to building wealth for retirement.

I left school at 16 and hitchhiked to the Gold Coast whilst Simon signed to play AFL with St Kilda. It was an exciting time for both of us. In 1980 I started working in real estate. I have to acknowledge my Jewish mentors who taught me not just the fundamentals of property but also the important difference of between '**simple and compound**' which transfers to '**Tactics and Strategy**'. In property this is the difference between **success and failure**. Simon outlines these fundamentals well in his thesis.

I have now been in the real estate business for over 45 years and still love what I do. I started coaching people when I built Custodian house in 1995, which sits on a 3 hectare campus on the Nerang River. One of the reasons we began public seminars and coaching was to bring awareness of our Toogoolawa program which is a school program for boys aged 8-15 that have been excluded from all mainstream schools.

Simon saw one of my presentations whilst he was working at Valvoline in 1997 and asked how he could learn to coach. He started working with us in 1998 when we set up our Melbourne client liaison office. He was a quick learner and with his coaching background able to introduce a foreign and complicated process to average Australians using the *7 Steps to Wealth* book (1st edition 1998) as the principal thesis. *7 Steps to Wealth* is now in its 9th edition and has been read by more than 500,000 Australians.

In early 2000's Simon went from managing the Melbourne client liaison office to operating it himself under a license agreement. He did really well and in 2008 he moved on to set up Logic Property Wealth Australia which is similar to the Custodian model without the delivery certainty (guarantees) or spread of location options.

Simons' a great coach and this thesis is a good document to highlight the difference between '**Tactic and Strategy**'. A good analogy comes from our mutual friend Barry Michael, former world boxing champion, who would say everyone has a 'winning tactic until they get punched in the head'. Strategy is to use the time and process of a proven formula. It's about working smarter not harder.

In Part A Simon covers some of the 'tactics' people use. In my 45 years of property, I've never met anyone who has successfully done any of those time and time again.

In Part B Simon introduces the 7 Steps Strategy of **compound growth**. I mentioned earlier that the *7 Steps to Wealth* book has been read by more than 500,000 Australians. The principal strategy is to build a portfolio of 10 or more investment properties. Today less than 3,000 Australians own 10 or more investment properties and many of them are Custodians. That's 0.6% of the people who have read 7 Steps.

Why?

There are lots of reasons but to do it you need the success mindset and the knowledge, skills and tools.

Simons' thesis covers the knowledge you will need, and he has coached enough people to point you in the right direction but, as with everything there's a big difference between knowing and doing and that's where it's up to you, the reader, to take action.

Simon's the guy to get you started.

John Fitzgerald

Introduction

Welcome to "The Logic of Property" proven methods of building wealth through Australian "Real" Estate".

In this book, I have divided it into two main sections. In section 1, we will explore time-tested strategies that have been instrumental in helping individuals across Australia achieve financial prosperity through real estate investment. These methods have been developed and refined over many years and specifically the past 28 years for myself as it has been that timeframe I have had in the residential investment industry. These methods have been used by myself and thousands of Australians through my companies, and particularly Logic Property Wealth Australia since 2008 resulting in significant wealth creation for many everyday Australians and over 2000 of my own clients.

Section two is more specific with some client case studies as well as some documentation I have written over the years that I make available for my client's education. These documents are more specific to what you need to know relating to investment in both personal, trusts and SMSF's. These documents are more relative to what we do at LPWA P/L but certainly can be used by yourself in your own endeavours. The main documentation is relative to clients' questions I have been asked over the years. I have answered these relative to LPWA P/L but again knowledge that all investors should understand.

At the helm of this insightful journey is me, Simon Meehan, the founder, and Director of Logic Property Wealth Australia P/L and LPWA Finance P/L a Mortgage Brokerage business with its focus on residential property for both owner occupied and investment in personal, trust and SMSF entities. Between both businesses, the combined expertise and experience, has helped thousands of individuals navigate the intricacies of real estate investment and specific and correct finance structuring, positioning them for long-term financial security and success in retirement.

The decision to focus exclusively on "real" estate, rather than property, is a deliberate one. Real estate, encompassing the land and its inherent value, serves as the foundation for sustainable wealth creation. Property, on the other hand, refers solely to the physical structures and depreciating assets. By homing in on "real" estate, we recognize the enduring appreciation of land as a fundamental driver of wealth, setting it apart from the mere building components that make up a property. This distinction is crucial in understanding the unique opportunities and advantages that real estate presents, especially in an Australian context where it represents more than just a tax- deductible asset. We at "Logic" pride ourselves on educating potential clients on the difference between Property and "Real" Estate. "Real Estate" is what you get a title for and that is land. **Land appreciates and buildings depreciate**!

Knowing this is a complete necessity if one wishes to build wealth in "**Real Estate**" in Australia.

In the pages that follow, we will delve into the methods that have been instrumental in our journey and the journeys of those clients we have worked with. These methods are designed to equip you with the knowledge and strategies necessary to harness the power of Australian real estate as a vehicle for wealth creation. Whether you are a seasoned investor or just beginning to explore the world of real estate, this book is your comprehensive guide to unlocking the full potential of real estate investment in Australia.

Prepare to embark on a transformative exploration of wealth-building strategies that have stood the test of time and have the potential to shape your financial future.. Welcome to "**The Logic of Property**" proven methods of building wealth through Australian "Real" Estate".

Who am I?

My name is Simon Henry Meehan. I was born in Bethlehem (well actually Bethlehem hospital, Caulfield, Melbourne, Victoria, Australia). I am the youngest of 9 children. Six boys and 3 girls.

I grew up in Brighton, a now affluent beach side suburb of Melbourne of which my family moved to from Geelong in 1870. Brighton was not the affluent suburb it is today back in the 1960's as most of the families at that time were large in number of kids. Our family was like most in the area. We played footy and cricket in the streets and would move off the road immediately at the call of "car".

Families of this time never had cash flow concerns because there wasn't any. We certainly didn't go without but there was not the available money as there seems to be in average families today.

My dad was a military man who served as an officer in the Australian Army Survey Corp, throughout the second world war. He spent much time away from home during the war in Darwin, New Guinea and the Pacific Islands. Apparently, he saw my older brother Bill for the first time when he was 18 months old. After the war, he maintained senior roles in the public service, finishing as the Victorian Chief Surveyor.

My mum was a Saint. She was the life of every party and passed on her love of life to all her nine children. She was a devout Catholic but never forced her beliefs onto others. Mum taught me that you must learn something new every day of your life.

All my siblings were educated at St Joan of Arc Catholic primary school in Brighton. My five children attended this school, and I still have my youngest son Freddie attending there now. Coincidentally my mum and dad meet there when the school was first opened in 1920.

My brothers and I all went to secondary school at CBC St Kilda where my dad had gone as well as my Grand Father and Great Grand Father. I am not sure that there would be too many other families anywhere in Australia that would have that type of family history at two schools.

My mum attended Presentation Convent Windsor which was across the road from CBC St Kilda. My sisters went to Star of the Sea in Gardenvale where my three daughters attended and two are attending now.

Some may suggest we haven't changed much in life! I have a beautiful wife Holly who as well as raising a family, controls most of our business marketing and financial affairs.

I was clever at school until my final few years where I didn't have much interest in anything other than sport and socialising. As a matter of fact, I was extremely good at both of those, especially the socialising.

Sport and partying were really all I cared about in senior school. Australian rules football and golf were my stand outs, although I did make the first eleven cricket team. Didn't make many runs as the opener, nor take many wickets bowling but I did take seven catches in one innings which I believe is some type of school ACC record.

I was offered an opportunity to become an assistant pro golfer at the age of 15 by the local professional at Brighton Golf Course. My father would have nothing of this as it was a must we all had a full formal education.

Australian Rules Football took priority for me after that, and it was here that I excelled. I won the best and fairest player in my last five years at school, two of these in the first eighteen, the last as Captain of the team which coincidentally won the prestigious Amco Herald Shield. This was the Victorian school boys' championships.

At the end of that year, I was recruited by St Kilda Football Club. In my first year I was promoted from the under 19's to the seconds for just two games before being promoted to the seniors and won the best first year player.

After five years of senior league football and at the ripe old age of 22, I gave it up. People ask me continuously why and all I can say it was a different time, and we were treated very differently than what the kids get today.

I did stay playing football at a lesser level for many years and had great success coaching in both Amateur and Country leagues.

My work life throughout these years was various pending football. I started as a junior sales cadet with S.P.C. (Shepparton Preserving Company). I had incredible mentors with my bosses being ex Campbell Soup sales guys who were at the top of the tree. I learnt so much in my 4-5 years with them. The most important thing being relationship selling to all clients.

My next main role was for many years in the oil industry with Valvoline, "you know what I mean"! again I worked with the best in the business and learnt so much in how to win a deal and hold onto it.

At the end of 1995, my good friend John Fitzgerald invited me to a presentation he was doing regarding investment property. I like most had zero idea in this field of business nor did I care. It wasn't until after this presentation that I realised that everyone needs to learn how to invest for themselves or a "poverty line" retirement is guaranteed. Harsh words but unfortunately true and still very true today.

It took some convincing but in 1997 I took on a role with John and his business as a Licensee of the Victorian operation of Custodian Wealth Builders. John released his book *7 Steps to Wealth* the following year and from that time our business took off significantly. The book basically exposed the industry and taught potential investors the difference between property and "REAL" estate. We taught people the basic fact that land appreciates, and buildings depreciate. We secured real estate assets for clients in growth areas all over the country and at the same time showed them how to gear and duplicate to give them the best chance of a quality retirement.

In 2008 I parted ways with CWB and started a new company trading as Logic Property Wealth Australia. My "criteria" is based on what John taught us many years before. Why? Because he was completely correct and a **proven method of success.**

Over the years I have seen many other marketing groups coming up with "better" ways of doing things and other get rich quick schemes. I am sure many have had success using those principals but know that the basics of buying land product in capital cities in affordable growth areas has stood the test of time and will continue to do so for many years after we have all gone. As they say "they ain't making any more land".

This book has been in the making for 16 years. I have continually written documents to give to my clients on subjects. Mainly they have been on questions that potential clients want and need to know. Regarding Finance and Valuations for investment and the necessity to understand why they differ so much from bank to bank. On the "criteria" for purchase every time as well as the three main questions one must ask and get answers for before buying each time.

Often people become bogged down on a particular subject and it stops them actioning. Unfortunately, that happens to many people and those persons will go nowhere. Why? The truth is they don't have specific goals with timelines forefront in their minds.

"He/She who is without goal is without direction". Nothing can be truer in life. So, people are happy to sit on their hands because they feel safe. Only those who act succeed. So don't be stopped or procrastinate because you don't know or understand something. Find the answer and move on.

I do hope this book delivers some answers that you may have been looking for. The simple answer to most is that you need a team around you. That's why clients work with us at LPWA P/L. We are connecting clients with everyone they need on their side to succeed. From property acquisition agents, land developers, builders, finance companies, lawyers, property managers, insurance agents, financial planners, building surveyors/ inspectors and quantity surveyors. The list goes on, but it is important you use the right people and have confidence they are on your team.

So, before you start reading this book, take some time and write down what you would like to achieve. Start with a dollar value of what you want in today's value per year for retirement. Then put down what year and specific date you wish to achieve this by.

Once you have done this and only when you have done this will things take shape and the knowledge you require will come to you.

If you do need help, then contact us at info@logicprop.com.au

Questions:

1. **In today's dollars, how much per year do I require each year in my retirement?**

____

2. **What is the exact date that I will retire and start to need these funds?**

____

Section 1

Chapter 1

Passive Wealth Building with Real Estate

Passive wealth building through real estate is a cornerstone of long-term financial security and prosperity. In this chapter, we will explore the "buy and hold strategy", a proven method that empowers individuals to leverage the enduring value of real estate for sustained wealth accumulation.

The "buy and hold strategy" is a straightforward yet powerful approach to real estate investment. It involves acquiring properties with the intention of holding onto them for an extended period, allowing their value to appreciate over time. Unlike more speculative or short-term investment strategies, buy and hold emphasizes the long-term ownership of real estate assets as a means to build wealth steadily and reliably. This method of wealth building is what I have been teaching and working with clients for the past 28 years. This "passive" strategy still requires much focus on what to buy, where to buy and how to buy.

Banks play a pivotal role in shaping an individual's capacity to engage in the buy and hold strategy. They assess an individual's borrowing capacity based on a variety of factors, including income, expenses, and existing financial commitments.

Understanding how banks control your capacity is crucial to successfully implementing the buy and hold strategy. Banks typically exercise caution by applying conservative valuations and imposing high buffers on top of standard variable rates when calculating borrowing capacity. Moreover, they consider living expenses as a key factor in determining the amount an individual can afford to borrow. One of the first things you must do if you intend to use this strategy is find out your maximum borrow capacity. The best way is to speak to a finance broker who can do these calculations and explain exactly how this is calculated and what the restrictions are with different banks policies. This is something worthwhile you understanding as there will be a need to "duplicate" and grow your asset base over time if you wish to reach your retirement goals. The biggest hurdle along the way is finance. Although it can cost you minimal amounts to hold "Real" Estate, the finance companies will not lend further unless under their criteria, you can afford to have more investment debt. Again, using a broker that can find you opportunities by understanding finance company's policies is a huge bonus.

The safety and security of the buy and hold method for long-term growth are evident in its conservative and strategic approach. By acquiring properties and holding onto them for extended periods, investors can benefit from the steady appreciation of "Real" estate values over time. This method provides a reliable and low-risk avenue for wealth accumulation, offering a level of safety and security that is often unmatched by more volatile investment strategies.

One of the key advantages of the "buy and hold strategy" is the potential to duplicate assets through revaluation. As properties increase in value over time, investors can leverage this appreciation to access additional capital. By revaluing existing assets and accessing increased equity, individuals can duplicate their assets, acquiring new properties or expanding their real estate portfolio without significant additional financial outlay.

Furthermore, it's important to understand the Loan-to-Value Ratio (LVR) that banks will allow you to go up to. LVR represents the percentage of the property value that a lender is willing to finance. While banks may impose certain limits on LVR, understanding these limits and working within them can empower investors to make informed decisions and maximize their borrowing capacity.

In summary, the buy and hold strategy stands as an exceptionally safe and reliable method for long-term wealth building through real estate. By understanding the role of banks in controlling borrowing capacity, leveraging property appreciation through revaluation, and recognizing the safety and security inherent in this method, individuals can position themselves for sustained wealth accumulation and financial prosperity.

Chapter 2

Active Trading in Real Estate.

Active trading in real estate encompasses a range of strategies where individuals actively participate in the buying, renovating, and selling of properties to generate profit. In this chapter, we will predominantly focus on the strategy of buying, renovating, and selling properties at a higher price, commonly known as property flipping. While this approach can yield substantial profits, it also carries inherent risks, making it essential for investors to carefully consider market conditions and financial implications.

Property flipping involves purchasing properties with the intention of renovating or improving them before selling at a higher price. This strategy is most viable in an upward-moving market, where property prices are on the rise. It is crucial for investors to be confident that market conditions will support a profitable sale price before committing to property flipping. Furthermore, an in-depth understanding of the local real estate market and trends is essential to mitigate risks and ensure a successful outcome.

One of the primary risks associated with property flipping is the potential for market downturns. In a declining or stagnant market, the anticipated profit margin may diminish or even become negative, resulting in financial loss. As such, property flipping is inherently tied to market conditions, and investors must exercise caution and diligence when assessing the feasibility of this strategy.

In addition to market risks, property flipping entails a range of costs that must be factored into the overall financial equation. These costs include buying expenses such as stamp duty, development costs, permits (if applicable), full renovation expenses, and selling costs, which also encompass Goods and Services Tax (GST). Understanding and accurately accounting for these costs is crucial in determining the potential profitability of a property flipping venture.

Another active trading approach in real estate involves buying off the plan and flipping the property prior to settlement and completion. This strategy involves purchasing a property before it is built or completed and then selling it before settlement, often with the intention of capitalizing on property price appreciation during the construction phase.

However, this approach also introduces unique risks, particularly in terms of financing. Banks may only offer conditional loans for off the plan purchases, as individuals' financial circumstances may change during the construction period. Additionally, upfront deposits are typically required for off the plan purchases, with the full payment due upon completion. Furthermore, loan offers from banks are usually valid for a limited period, typically around three months, adding a time-sensitive dimension to the financing aspect of off the plan property flipping.

Many speculative investors were involved with the strategy during the boom times of the 1970's and 80's on The Gold Coast and other areas. When an apartment block was completed, it was common to see multi sales on one apartment that changed hands many times at this time of settlement. If you intend to be involved with this type of strategy and projects, then you need to ensure that there will be someone around that will buy the property from you at a higher price.

In summary, active trading in real estate offers opportunities for substantial profit, but it also carries inherent risks that must be carefully evaluated and managed. Whether through property flipping or off the plan purchases, investors must thoroughly assess market conditions, financial implications, and associated risks to make informed decisions and maximize the potential for success in active real estate trading.

Chapter 3

Buy, Demolish, and Build: Real Estate Development in Australia.

In this chapter, we will delve into the process of buying, demolishing, and building on properties in Australia, exploring the various factors involved, timelines to consider, costs, financing options, risks, council regulations, and the potential of selling "off the plan." Again, this is another form of "active" investment.

Undertaking a buy, demolish, and build project in Australia is a substantial endeavour that requires careful planning and execution. The timeline for such a project can vary depending on factors such as the size of the development, council approval processes, construction timelines, and any unforeseen delays. Typically, the process can take several months to several years from acquisition to completion, with each stage requiring meticulous attention to detail.

The costs involved in a buy, demolish, and build project can be significant and may include expenses such as property acquisition costs, demolition costs, design and construction costs, council fees, utility connections, landscaping, and more. It is crucial to conduct thorough cost assessments and budgeting to ensure the financial viability of the project from start to finish.

Financing a real estate development project of this nature can be achieved through various avenues, including traditional bank loans, construction loans, private financing, joint ventures, or a combination of these. It is important to explore different financing options, assess their terms and conditions, and choose the most suitable option that aligns with the project's financial requirements and timeline.

Risks associated with buy, demolish, and build projects include cost overruns, construction delays, market fluctuations, regulatory challenges, and unforeseen issues during the development process. Mitigating these risks involves thorough due diligence, engaging experienced professionals, obtaining the necessary approvals, and having contingency plans in place to address unexpected challenges that may arise.

Councils play a crucial role in determining what can be built on a particular block of land through zoning regulations, planning guidelines, building codes, and development approvals. Understanding and complying with council requirements is essential in ensuring that the proposed development aligns with local regulations and policies.

Selling "off the plan" involves marketing and selling properties before they are built or completed, offering buyers the opportunity to purchase based on plans and specifications. While selling off the plan can have benefits such as locking in a purchase price and potential capital growth, it also carries risks such as changes in market conditions, delays in construction, and variations in the final product compared to initial expectations. Whether selling off the plan is a positive or negative strategy depends on various factors, including market dynamics, buyer demand, project timelines, and risk tolerance.

In conclusion, embarking on a buy, demolish, and build project in Australia requires careful consideration of timelines, costs, financing options, risks, council regulations, and the potential of selling off the plan. By conducting thorough research, engaging with experienced professionals, and implementing a strategic approach, investors can navigate the complexities of real estate development and maximize the success of their projects. One very important point in using this strategy is ensuring you have a solicitor that has knowledge and expertise in property law.

Chapter 4:

Adding a New Build, Developing Land, and Splitting Blocks.

In this chapter, we will explore the process of adding a new residence to an existing dwelling, developing englobo land or dividing existing blocks, discussing planning considerations, council requirements, guidelines, necessary approvals, expertise, costs, and financing options.

Adding a new residence to an existing dwelling involves extending or building an additional dwelling on the same property. To undertake this project, careful planning is essential to meet council requirements, zoning regulations, and building codes. Council guidelines and requirements can typically be obtained from the local council's planning department or website, outlining specific regulations, restrictions, and procedures for property development in the area.

Developing land englobo or dividing existing blocks involves subdividing land to create new lots or allotments. This process requires obtaining various approvals, including subdivision approval, planning permits, and building permits. Seeking advice from qualified experts such as town planners, surveyors, architects, and legal professionals is crucial to navigate the complexities of land development and ensure compliance with regulatory requirements.

The costs associated with adding a new build, developing land, or splitting blocks can vary depending on factors such as land size, location, development complexity, council fees, professional fees, construction costs, infrastructure requirements, and utility connections. Conducting a thorough cost analysis and budgeting exercise is essential to determine the financial feasibility of the project and ensure that all expenses are accounted for.

In terms of financing, banks may provide loans or financing options to support property development projects, including adding a new build or subdividing land. However, the bank's willingness to finance the operation will depend on factors such as the project's viability, financial projections, feasibility studies, and the borrower's financial standing. Banks may require detailed project plans, cost estimates, and timelines to assess the risk and potential return on investment.

When seeking financing for property development projects, it is advisable to work with experienced mortgage brokers or financial advisors who specialize in real estate development financing. These professionals can help navigate the lending process, explore financing options, negotiate terms, and secure the most suitable financing arrangement for the project.

In summary, adding a new build, developing land, or splitting blocks can be lucrative property development ventures that offer the potential for capital growth and increased property value. By understanding council requirements, obtaining necessary approvals, seeking expert advice, estimating costs accurately, and exploring financing options, investors can successfully undertake and complete property development projects while maximizing their return on investment.

Chapter 5

Buying in Regional Markets.

In this chapter, we will delve into the dynamics of buying property in regional markets in Australia, exploring the historical trends, growth factors, and vulnerabilities that differentiate these markets from capital cities.

Traditionally, regional markets in Australia have not exhibited the same level of growth in median home prices as capital cities. There are several factors contributing to this disparity, with one key reason being the difference in demand drivers between regional areas and capital cities. Capital cities typically offer a more diverse range of employment opportunities, amenities, services, infrastructure, and lifestyle options compared to regional areas. This higher level of economic activity and population density in capital cities often translates into stronger demand for housing, leading to higher property price growth over time.

Regional markets are more susceptible to fluctuations in specific employment conditions, industries, or economic factors that can impact property values. When major employers in regional areas experience downturns, closures, or relocations, it can result in a significant exodus of residents seeking employment opportunities elsewhere. This sudden outflow of population can lead to decreased demand for housing in regional markets, causing property prices to stagnate or decline.

The lack of demand in regional markets, particularly in comparison to capital cities, is closely tied to the number and variety of job opportunities available. Capital cities are economic hubs with diverse industries, a concentration of businesses, government institutions, educational facilities, cultural amenities, and infrastructure that attract a large and varied workforce. This concentration of economic activity and job opportunities creates a high demand for housing in capital cities, supporting property price growth and investment potential.

In contrast, regional markets may have a more limited job market, with fewer industries or sectors driving economic growth and employment. The lower population density and limited diversity of job opportunities in regional areas can result in lower demand for housing, slower population growth, and reduced property price appreciation compared to capital cities. Additionally, the lack of essential services, amenities, and infrastructure in some regional areas may further contribute to the lower demand for property in these markets.

In summary, the differences in demand drivers, economic factors, and job opportunities between regional markets and capital cities play a significant role in shaping property price growth and investment potential. While regional markets offer unique lifestyle advantages and affordability, they are often more susceptible to economic fluctuations, job market changes, and demand volatility compared to capital cities. Understanding these dynamics is essential for investors considering buying property in regional markets to make informed decisions and mitigate risks associated with regional market conditions.

Personally, I acknowledge that some people have done very well with Real estate in regional markets. I learn't quickly that regional markets can be dangerous pending economic situations. Most regional markets rely upon one main form of employment. If something was to happen to that main employment organisation, then it would have a negative effect on the residential market as people would need to migrate elsewhere for employment. An example of this was Newcastle in the mid 90's. BHP decided to move from Newcastle, and it left many unemployed.

We know that the average household in Australia has around 2.7 people living in it. When Ford closed their doors in Geelong there were also many left unemployed and needed to move to seek new employment. The best example of regional markets being dangerous is North Queensland and the mining areas. We have seen mines start up and require serious amounts of housing for the people taking up the lucrative jobs available. Unfortunately, we have also seen mines close which means these people have lost their jobs and hence no longer any need for accommodation. I had clients of mine invest in such areas in the 1990's and 2000's. As much as I warned them against doing so, they jumped in buying homes at $300,000. These properties within 2-3 years had jumped to $800,000 and were renting at $1000 per week. Shortly after the mine closed and today, they are stuck with debt and cannot sell them for even $100,000.

So, you can do well if you buy and sell at the exact correct times. Just be careful and be confident that this type of thing is unlikely to happen. For me and all my LPWA P/L clients, I stick to a Capital City with above 1 million in population each and every time. This does not guarantee me immediate Capital growth but because of the multiple forms of employment, tenants have always a better chance of being employed and an ability to pay my rent. There will always be demand for my property and as we know the demand has never been stronger in Australia's history for house and land product because of our continually growing population. Demand and growth can only come from an area that has guaranteed continual opportunities with employment.

Chapter 6

Inheriting Property

Inheriting property obviously has significant benefits, but it also comes with costs and considerations. There is obviously a difference between "building" wealth and "inheriting" wealth.

Inheriting property can provide financial security and stability by eliminating the need to pay rent or a mortgage. Real estate properties tend to appreciate over time, so inheriting property can be a valuable asset that grows in value and adds to your own wealth base.

Inheriting a family home or property can hold sentimental value and help preserve family legacy. It can also be used, if sold to help pay off your own mortgage and or debts.

Depending on the jurisdiction, you may need to pay inheritance taxes on the property you inherit. However, inheritance tax laws vary widely by country and region. It is worthwhile discussing these things with your accountant or financial advisor prior to inheritance. This will ensure you understand completely what rules and requirements you must adhere to.

Owning a property comes with maintenance costs, property taxes, insurance, and potential renovation expenses.

If you sell an inherited property, you may be subject to capital gains tax on the difference between the selling price and the fair market value at the time of inheritance.

The tax liability usually falls on the person who inherits and sells the property.

Gifting Property While Alive:

If a property is gifted to you while the owner is still alive, gift tax may apply depending on the value of the property and local tax laws.

Gifting a property while alive can have implications for the owner's financial situation, taxes, and potential Medicare eligibility.

Before making any decisions regarding inheritance, gifting, or leveraging family equity, it's essential to consult with a financial advisor or legal professional to fully understand the implications and risks involved.

Chapter 7

Using Parents Equity and or grants.

Using parents' equity or being gifted money for housing in Australia can be a strategy to help you enter the property market or upgrade to a larger home. There are some key points to consider before entering into such an agreement that both parties must understand completely.

Parents can provide equity in their home that you can use as a deposit or collateral for a home loan. Banks will differ with their policies pending different circumstances and "strength" of main borrowers' serviceability.

Lenders will assess your ability to repay the loan, as well as the equity available in your parents' property.

If you default on the loan, it could put your parents' home at risk of foreclosure. It's essential to have a clear agreement in place with your parents outlining the terms of the equity arrangement.

Being Gifted Money for Housing:

Parents can gift money to use as a deposit for a home purchase. In Australia, gifts are generally not taxed, but there may be tax implications if the gift is considered a loan.

It's important to document the gift properly to avoid any confusion or legal issues in the future and it must be noted it is not repayable.

Most lenders will require a gift letter to confirm that the money is a gift and not a loan.

First Homeowner Grants.

First-time homebuyers in Australia may be eligible for First Homeowner Grants and stamp duty concessions, which can help reduce the cost of buying a home.

The eligibility criteria for these benefits vary by state and territory. They also change over time as most grants are only put in place for a certain period of time.

Guarantors:

Some lenders offer guarantor loans where a family member, usually a parent, guarantees the loan using their property as security.

Guarantors are taking on the risk that they may have to cover the loan repayments if the borrower defaults. Both the borrower and the guarantor should seek legal advice before entering into a guarantor arrangement.

Before using parents' equity or accepting a gift for housing in Australia, it's crucial to understand the legal and financial implications. Consulting with a financial advisor or a mortgage broker can help you navigate the process and make informed decisions that align with your financial goals.

Chapter 8:

Parents as Guarantors.

Having parents act as guarantors for their children's home loans can be a way to help them enter the property market, but it also comes with risks for both parties. Here are some of the risks involved in parents being guarantors for their children's home loans:

1. Financial Risk for Parents:

If the child defaults on the loan or is unable to make repayments, the parents as guarantors are liable to cover the outstanding amount. This can put the parents' own assets, including their home, at risk.

Parents may need to sell their own property or use their savings to repay the loan, potentially affecting their own financial stability and retirement plans.

2. Strained Relationships:

Financial disagreements or the stress of loan repayments can strain the relationship between parents and their children. Defaults on loan repayments can lead to tension and conflict within the family.

3. Impact on Parents' Credit Score:

If the child defaults on the loan and the parents as guarantors are required to step in, it can negatively impact the parents' credit score. This can make it more challenging for them to access credit in the future.

4. Limited Financial Flexibility:

Acting as a guarantor ties up the parents' borrowing capacity, making it more difficult for them to secure their own loans or credit in the future. This can affect their ability to access credit for their own needs.

5. Legal Obligations:

Parents need to fully understand their legal obligations as guarantors, including the extent of their liability and the potential consequences if the child defaults on the loan.

6. Market Fluctuations:

If the property market experiences a downturn or the value of the property decreases, the equity available to cover the loan may diminish. This can increase the financial risk for both the child and the parents.

Before agreeing to become guarantors for their children's home loans, parents should carefully assess their own financial situation, seek independent legal and financial advice, and have open and honest discussions with their children about the implications and risks involved. It's essential for both parties to have a clear understanding of the responsibilities and potential outcomes before proceeding with a guarantor arrangement.

What are the risks involved with parents being guarantors for children wanting home loans?

Although most would consider these risks minimal, it is Imperative that both parties recognise that there are definite risks.

By being a "Guarantor" for family or someone else when purchasing property, in most cases means offering security of another asset (usually parents' home) is used to secure the new buy. It can also mean that the guarantor is using their income to also help with the purchase. If the main person borrowing gets into financial difficulty and is unable to make monthly payments, then the guarantor must come good with the continued payments. If the guarantor is at that stage unable or not willing to make payments any longer, then the property will be a "forced" sale. This does have concerns as banks can take possession and force a sale within 90 days. There is often not solid and continual marketing to sell as one would normally do, and the bank will sell the property at the specified date no matter what the circumstances. This means that they may sell for less than the original purchase price. If it is drastically below the original purchase price, like with a lot of apartment type property, then the bank takes their borrowed amount first and the difference is repaid back to the guarantor or main borrower. If the property is sold for less than the bank's borrowed amount, and less than what the original deposit was, then the bank has the right to sue both the main borrower and the guarantor for that difference.

This is how we have seen parents in the past lose the family home. It is a rare occasion but has happened and anyone considering this needs to know these risks.

The obvious main risk is the "borrowers and guarantor" not understanding "Real Estate" and buying a "Property" that has the chance of going down in value. This happens when the buyers pay too much initially for "property" and generally with units and high-rise apartments. These types of properties have minimal land value and as discussed, many times, it is only the land that appreciates, and all buildings depreciate and go down in value.

Even if a person does buy this property and even if the value does drop, they only can get in trouble if they cannot make the repayments or if it is an investment, if they are without tenants and hence cash flow to hold the property. The banks will eventually want the property sold and take possession to sell in a "fire sale" type of scenario".

Because the banks have taken in most cases a 20% deposit, they have a decent buffer whereby they rarely lose. If the property sells for what the purchase price was then all will receive their money back and be happy. If it sells for less, then the bank takes the money owed first and will pay back the rest appropriately. If it sells for less than what the buyer has put down as a deposit, or the guarantor has "lent" as security from equity of another asset, then no money is returned and hence the parents who have "guaranteed" and usually lent the children the deposit funds, will lose all of this amount and potentially be sued by the finance company for the extra difference.

Section 2

Section 2

Chapter 1

Criteria for Purchase and Duplication.

The LPWA P/L "Criteria for Duplication" has two components with focus on Capital Growth and Cash Flow.

By maintaining focus on each of these points it takes the emotion out of every investment decision and puts the "LOGIC" into the exercise.

Most people get dragged into each purchase with emotion of the buy. "I wouldn't live here" is a common sentence that I hear often from potential clients. You may not live there but the question is and more important is will someone else "always" want to live there? Is there and will there be continual demand for your property. Are the six reason why people choose to live where they live in Australia met? Is the rent required and achievable affordable for every person in this country that rents?

Capital Growth:

The reasons why people in Australia choose to live where they live?

1. **Schools**
2. **Family/Security**
3. **Transport**
4. **Shopping Centres**
5. **Jobs/Employment**
6. **Recreation**

We want all properties to be within 5kms of all these main points of demand criteria. Sticking to a Capital City with above $1 million in population near guarantees us meeting these points of criteria.

To get even more specific, we need to break down these points even further.

1. **Schools-** how many schools are located close? Public? Private? Primary?

2. **Family/Security-** is 70% of the suburb owner occupied? Is there above the average of 2.7 people per household? What is the medium family income of the suburb? Average age of the area is also important. Will the people living there be adding children to the area? Will their average

income increase as they stay and get older? Will they be adding value to their property by adding on rooms or adding in a swimming pool?

3. **Transport -** what is the road system like in this suburb? (Australian's predominantly drive cars). Where is the public transport? Trains? Buses? Trams?

4. **Shopping Centres -** Is there a major shopping complex within 5km from the suburb?

5. **Jobs/Employment -** Again a Capital City with above 1 million population will give us multi forms of employment.

6. **Recreation -** where will kids play? Are there football grounds/soccer/cricket other sporting facilities nearby? Golf courses, tennis courts etc.

In Australia we tend to have an abundance of these amenities but the more there is nearby the stronger the demand.

Interesting to note that Australian's are happy to travel up to an hour to get to work but want their kids within 5 minutes of school or have easy access via public transport to get there.

Land Content:

The Land Content Value (LCV) must be a minimum of 30% the total investment.

Preferably even higher percentage but 30% of a new buy should at least be sufficient for you to obtain the average growth that the medium house will give over the next 10 years.

How do we work out what the (LCV) is of a particular piece of Real estate?

Every "property' has a value and has two components that make up the value?

1. **The land value.**

2. **The value of the improvements.**

If you are buying off the plan a house and land package, you will most likely be signing two contracts. One for the land and the other with a builder for the construction of the house.

There will be a price for both the build and the land. If I want to know the real value of what it is worth today, you just need to work out what a square meter of land is worth in that area and multiply by the size of the block you are about to purchase. There are many factors that can influence the value like which way it sits on the block, is it a hilly block that may need a lot of land cutting or a pole home to be built.

Usually land developers will have a price list and able to show you what land in the estate is selling for at that time. They very seldom drop land prices and in today's climate the demand for land has never been higher.

The house/property being constructed will vary in price pending many factors. The size of the house, the quality of construction and fittings. What type of product is being used to build, the type of roof, fencing, driveway, landscaping and much more. In truth you must compare "apples with apples" but we can quite simply get a good idea if what I am paying is on the mark for construction at that time.

There is nothing else for you to find out once you have these two important components. Land and Improvements.

Remember that this price may not be reflected by a bank's valuation on the property as they are calling on the valuation to be done for "security" purposes. **Their security!**

Logic Property Wealth Australia - Criteria for Duplication

Duplication

Capital Growth

Cash Flow

DEMOGRAPHICS

- Stick to a capital city with a population above 1 Million.
- Average number of people per household (3+).
- Average income per household- preferably above $1500 per week.
- % of owner occupiers in suburb (above 70%)
- Median Age.

GROWTH CRITERIA

HPV – Higher Property Values

-Existing or guaranteed

Demand Criteria:

1. Schools
2. Family/Security.
3. Transport
4. Shopping Centres
5. Jobs
6. Recreation

-**Land Content Value** (**LCV**) must be a minimum of 30% of Total Investment.

FINANCE

-Understand the valuation to be used by your lending institution and know what amount of security is been used.

-Borrow 100% plus costs (Interest only)

-Lending institution must use minimum 80% projected rental income in assessment.

-90% Bank Loan if required each and every time if correct for your structure.

-No Cross Collateralization.

-Understand each banks loan to value (LVR) ratio for each type of dwelling. (Apartment V House)

-Recognize the Debt to Service Ratio (DSR) calculation for every specific purchase.

RELIABLE INCOME

-Must have a Taxable Income (Max tax deductions).

-Minimum Weekly outlay (Within your Budget).

-Less than 30% of Investors in suburb.

-Insurance – Building & Contents, Landlord Protection, Rental (if available).

-Rent $500 - $800 per week.

-Vacancy Rate – Less than 3%.

-Always employ a Licensed Property Manager.

THE DWELLING

- Ensure you use a reliable and registered builder.

-100% Guaranteed Fixed Price Contract. (No Variations)

-Must be brand new each and every time.

-Designed for Renters.

-Specifically chosen to meet individual personal scenario & goals.

TAX DEDUCTIONS

-Claim all Tax Deductions.

-Brand New Property.

-Maximum Depreciation.

-Obtain Quantity Surveyors Report.

TIMING & CYCLES

-Understand areas cycle at different times and vary in length.

-Buy with the view of holding for a minimum of one full cycle.

-Ensure growth in first half of cycle (view recent history of property).

-Buy at the bottom of the market.

-Ensure affordability.

LPWA ensure that every property that a client purchases meet this above strict criteria and are personally selected with your end goal in mind. Getting just one of these criteria incorrect, could possibly set you back years in achieving your goal… You cannot afford to get this wrong.

Chapter 2.

Real v Perceived Growth.

What we are discussing here is the dynamics of the real estate market and how pricing and sales are influenced by various factors. We need to be always careful of what is "actual" and what is projected or predicted.

Statistical Increase vs. Real-time Prices.

Statistical forecasts of price increases in an area do not guarantee that new deals made at current prices will see the same percentage increase in the same period. Prices may have already been adjusted to account for projected growth.

Timing of Sales recording is very much the reason for differences in statistics of actual Sales of house and land products. These "packages" may be contracted immediately but not settled until much later when titles are obtained. This delay in settlement means that sales are not recorded by relevant authorities until a future date. This can have a huge differentiation in valuations for banks security purposes. Valuers must use "sales" that have occurred, settled, and documented by the

Valuer Generals Department and they will not use "first" time sales in new estates but resales that have occurred in the previous twelve-month period.

No land developer will sell land for less than what they know they can achieve. So, these actual sales are real but not yet justified in sales data as they haven't settled.

There is always a continual Impact of Demand on Pricing. When a release of house and land product sells out, vendors usually increase prices for the next release due to this demand. Buyers contracting at the new prices will not benefit from the same pricing as those who contracted earlier. This is the main reason why developers only release a small number of blocks for each release. They have an ability because of demand to increase the land prices per release.

When we look at long-term growth considerations, we need to emphasize the LPWA P/L criteria for investment purchases.

The LPWA P/L "Criteria for Duplication," provides a more secure and risk-averse approach to achieving growth and cash flow in the real estate market. The focus for long term Capital growth is ensuring 30-40% of the initial investment is the land value component and for reliable Cash Flow ensuring the demand for tenancy and as such the rents required are affordable for all tenants.

Be careful of statements suggesting "Guaranteed Increase" in Medium House Price Growth of a particular area. The guaranteed increase in medium house price growth in the next 12 months is attributed to sales that have already been completed, with prices reflecting the anticipated growth at the time of contracting. These figures will come to fruition as they have already been made, but as discussed it does not guarantee that you as a new purchaser can get the same price as someone who has already contracted but awaiting settlement because titles on the land have not been issued.

This is a genuine concern when stated for units and apartments.

Having an investment structure and Investment Strategy is critical for success. Considering proven criteria for long-term growth and cash flow, as well as understanding the dynamics of pricing, demand, and sales timing, will help investors make informed decisions in the real estate market.

It's important for investors to conduct thorough research, consider various factors influencing the market, and adopt a long-term investment strategy to navigate the complexities of the real estate market effectively.

Please see on page 48 the LPWA P/L "Criteria for Duplication" which has two components of focus, Capital Growth and Cash Flow.

By maintaining focus on each of these points it takes the emotion out of every investment and puts the "LOGIC" into the exercise.

Chapter 3

Financing in Trusts

When it comes to obtaining finance for a trust to purchase real estate in Australia, banks generally follow specific policies and considerations. It is extremely important that you choose the correct entity to purchase real estate. There are many factors that decide what entity you should be purchasing within. If you are considering building a portfolio of properties, then it would be wise to investigate the benefits of doing this by having separate trusts as the holding entities. Check that your finance broker understands these benefits as they can be significant. If you do want more explanation of the benefits, then contact us at Logic Property Wealth Australia Finance P/L. It is wise to seek independent financial advice on what entity you should use before purchasing.

Here is some valuable information regarding trusts and financing with trusts:

1. **Trust Structure:** Banks evaluate the type of trust (e.g., discretionary, unit, or hybrid) and require detailed documentation, including the trust deed, to understand the trust's structure and the role of trustees and beneficiaries.

2. **Trustee's Role:** Since the trustee is the legal owner of the property, lenders assess the trustee's creditworthiness. They often but not always require a personal guarantee from trustees or directors of the corporate trustee.

3. **Serviceability and Loan Terms:** The bank will assess the trust's ability to service the loan as it does with individuals, which may involve evaluating the income of the trust's assets and the financial standing of guarantors. Trust loans may come with stricter conditions, such as higher interest rates or lower loan-to-value ratios.

4. **Additional Security:** Banks might require additional security, including cross-collateralization with other trust or personal assets. Different banks have different criteria which definitely creates different outcomes of borrowing levels.

It is also worth investigating information regarding having a geared property in one trust and borrowing for a separate trust:

Separate Entities: Trusts are generally considered separate entities for lending purposes. Having a geared property in one trust does not automatically restrict another trust from borrowing, provided each trust has its distinct structure and independence in operation and assets.

Guarantors and Shared Debt: If the same individuals are acting as guarantors for both trusts, the bank will consider their total financial exposure. High levels of debt or gearing in one trust might impact the borrowing capacity of guarantors, affecting the ability of a separate trust to secure financing. Again, banks have different policies, and it is worth investigating exactly what is possible with different banks.

Overall Financial Health: Lenders will review the overall financial health of the involved parties and any interconnectedness between trusts. They may take a holistic view of the financial standing, especially if the trusts share beneficiaries or trustees. Again, banks policies differ from one bank to the next and it is worth investigating what can be achieved using different financial entities.

Ultimately, while separate trusts can potentially obtain finance independently, individual circumstances and the financial profiles of trustees and guarantors play a significant role. Consulting with financial advisors or mortgage brokers familiar with trust structures can provide personalized guidance in navigating these lending scenarios.

Chapter 4

Purchasing property within a Self-Managed Super Fund

Purchasing property within a Self-Managed Super Fund (SMSF) in Australia can be a smart investment strategy, but there are specific rules and considerations to keep in mind:

1. **Purpose and Compliance:** The property must align with the sole purpose of providing retirement benefits to the fund members. It shouldn't be for personal use by you or related parties. That means property like beach houses are NOT allowed to be purchased inside the SMSF. It is also imperative that the purchase is a one contract buy. That means that a property that is to be constructed, cannot be "purchased" until it is completed. This means that a builder needs to fund the construction until completed. A contract can be done whereby a deposit is paid but settlement does not happen until completion. Of course, an already established old property meets this requirement.

2. **Types of Property:** SMSFs can purchase residential or commercial properties, but residential properties cannot be lived in by a fund member or related party. However, commercial properties can be leased to a fund member's business, as long as it's at market rates.

3. **Borrowing Rules:** If your SMSF needs to borrow to purchase a property, it must be done under a Limited Recourse Borrowing Arrangement (LRBA). The loan can only be secured against the single asset purchased with the borrowed funds. A bare trust needs to be set up as this becomes the borrowing entity. A financial planner can control this structure being set up correctly and conforming with ASIC regulations.

4. **Investment Strategy:** Ensure the purchase aligns with the SMSF's investment strategy, which should outline the fund's objectives and asset allocation plans. A lending institution will require a S.O.A. (statement of advice) from a licensed financial planner before approving finance for the purchase. This is another ASIC requirement to ensure you have sourced qualified advice prior to commitment. The S.O.A. will act like a finance health check as financial planners are required to advise on correct insurance amounts required as well as stating why this investment is a good thing to do.

5. **Fund Liabilities:** Consider how the property purchase will impact the SMSF's liquidity and ability to cover liabilities, such as taxes and fees.

As with any investment, it is important to know the cashflow implications. Purchasing a property inside a SMSF is no different and it is imperative that you understand what amounts of costs will be required to cover everything associated with the property as well as knowing where those funds will come from.

6. **Costs and Management:** Factor in all associated costs, such as stamp duty, legal fees, property management fees, and potential renovations or maintenance. It is wise to do a full analysis of yearly costs and to be overly conservative to ensure all these are covered.

7. **Tax Implications:** Rental income from the property is taxed at the concessional rate of 15%, and capital gains are discounted significantly if the property is held for more than 12 months. The significant benefit of property sold from within a SMSF in retirement is that there is zero Capital Gains paid at this time.

8. **Regulatory and Compliance Requirements:** Ensure compliance with the Australian Taxation Office (ATO) and the Superannuation Industry (Supervision) Act 1993. Keeping comprehensive records is critical. Having a reputable financial advisor and competent accountant is critical. All funds must be audited each year under ASIC regulations.

9. **Professional Advice:** Given the complexity, it's wise to consult with financial advisors, tax professionals, or SMSF specialists to ensure compliance and maximize benefits. SMSF's are a growing entity amongst the community and have significant benefits if done and controlled correctly by these professionals.

Remember, managing an SMSF requires diligence and understanding of the regulations to ensure the fund's operations are compliant and beneficial for your retirement planning.

Explanation of SMSF purchasing procedure (with LPWA P/L).

- LPWA P/L finds you a suitable product that meets ASIC requirements and our LPWA P/L criteria.
- To secure a Real Estate package we must do an EOI (Expression of Interest). This costs you $1000 which is used in settlement or refunded if you don't proceed.
- Contract is drawn up and sent to solicitor for checking over (solicitor checks to ensure subject to finance). Unfortunately, in most cases the buying entity (Bare Trust) will not be set up at this time. The contract cannot be signed or countersigned by Vendor until the correct buying entity is set up correctly.

- The independent Financial Planner we recommend clients to, needs to be instructed to move forward in getting this trust and entity set up.

- The Bare Trust (Buying Entity) cannot be fully set up until a property has been chosen. The Bare Trust must designate the address of the property to be purchased.

- Most contracts are now signed via DocuSign (electronically). Once signed the lawyer will pass it back to vendor for counter signing.

- The lawyer will then send it back to the broker who needs this counter signed contract for finance application. Contracts are signed "subject to finance".

- Deposits cannot be paid until your SMSF has funds in its bank account. This means the Financial Planner must have set up the SMSF and hence received an ABN from ATO before the bank account for the fund can be put in place. Obviously, the bank account must be set up before monies from Managed Funds can be rolled over into your SMSF account. The Financial Planner must have also set up the Bare Trust which is the buying entity. Once all of this has been done the deposits can be paid and you are unconditional on the purchase.

- For SMSF purchases, full finance approval cannot be obtained until the property has been completed and valued. We do get a conditional loan approval based on your circumstances with the "condition" that the property is completed as in contract and valued as such.

- There is zero other money paid after deposit until property is complete and settlement occurs.

Case Study: SMSF Purchase:

- John and Mary are 45 years of age.
- They have $350k combined in managed Funds.
- The property costs $800k with a rental income of $700 per week.
- Broker applies for a 70% Non Recourse loan.
- Other costs are property management fees, insurance and rates approx. $5000 per year.
- Total holding costs $50,000 per year.
- Rent $700 x 52 = $36,400.
- Work contributions approx. $18,900.
- This money can be used to reduce the mortgage balance or invested elsewhere under advice from Financial Planner.

Why purchasing a house and land product in a newly set up SMSF is a great idea:

1. Avoid the risk of a meltdown crash of the stock market that happens on average every 7-8 years.

2. The security of bricks and mortar on LAND.

3. Tax benefits in retirement.

4. No tax on the income/rent derived from the property and taken out of the fund used for retirement.

5. The comparison of the House and Land product v Managed funds is outstanding. Using conservative growth and income figures our financial advisor has shown the average client is $4-$500,000 better off over a 12–15-year period.

6. Effectively your rental income, tax return and yearly work contributions from employer pays all costs to hold and pay down the debt.

7. Your Super money pays for all set up costs of the new SMSF, the required Bare Trust Statement of Advice completed by Financial Advisor (required by lending institution), bank fees, legal fees and any other set up costs.

Over the past 50 years, the Australian Stock Market has experienced several significant downturns. Here are the years when it notably crashed or saw significant declines:

1. **1987 - The Black Monday crash** in October affected markets worldwide, including Australia.

2. **1997 - The Asian Financial Crisis** led to downturns in many markets.

3. **2000 - The Dot-com bubble** burst affected global markets, including Australia.

4. **2008 - The Global Financial Crisis** saw significant declines in markets around the world.

5. **2020 - The COVID-19 pandemic** led to a sharp and sudden market crash in March.

- These are some of the major downturns, but markets can experience smaller corrections or periods of volatility as well.

- "Real Estate" in Australia rarely goes down in value and hence why so many people are looking to secure within a SMSF.

Chapter 5

The Logic of Property Valuations and Property Finance

LPWA (Logic Property Wealth Australia) P/L have licensed finance brokers that we refer and work with to fully help with our client's financial requirement. All these businesses are individually owned and separate from LPWA P/L.

Having the right finance structure for Wealth Building and Duplication is not just a good thing, but a critical element.

As a matter of fact, if you don't structure your finance correctly it is impossible for you to build wealth and achieve your financial goals.

Why should I use a broker?

There seems to be no LOGIC in the fact that even though it may cost me very little to hold a property, it may even be positive with income and tax benefits, yet the bank won't give you a loan.

Why? Why not? How can this be?

Finance company's lending criteria changes continuously and very much differs from bank to bank. However, the basics of the criteria have been in place for over a hundred years. In simple terms, you need a deposit, and you need serviceability. In other words, you must be capable of servicing the repayments.

Traditionally the banks look at your gross income and say one third is used for tax, one third for living and that leaves another third "only" that can be used for paying mortgage or rent. As well as this they may or may not use a proportion of the projected rent. They will focus on other "extra" expenses such as children, limit of credit cards and of course any other loans or financial commitments.

Banks control the affordability of property!

Property markets run for a limited time, purely based on demand. The demand is controlled by the allowance of the banks in what they will consider clients can borrow.

The controlling of affordability of property is done via several ways but simply put it is stringently controlled by the amounts the banks will lend!

We should remember that the banks need to lend to make money. They are conscious of providing annual dividends for their shareholders, but also continuously conscious of their exposure to risk. Therefore, we see individual banks' lending criteria continually moving and either becoming more stringent or more relaxed.

Everything in life cycles!

The banking finance industry is no different. Depending on what time it is on the economic clock, will depend on how easy or difficult it is to obtain a loan. It can also vary from bank to bank and how much "exposure" that bank may have to that asset class or even that area, suburb or development.

Currently, we see the banks as tight on lending as they have been for 50+ years. It's a strange scenario but because we have had 13 consecutive rate rises before our first 0.25% drop in April 2025. Interestingly our rates in June 2025 are still 1.00% lower than the 30-year average! Also considering we are coming off the lowest interest rates we've seen for over 80 years.

The 2008 GFC saw a property bust in the USA. Their banking system is very different from ours as the Australian Finance Industry is **extremely regulated**. In the USA most loans were unsecured and non-recourse, which meant house owners could throw their house keys on the banks counter and not be forced to honour the existing finance loan. We do not have that available to us.

Australia's financial industry is heavily regulated and those "non-recourse" loans are only available for SMSF and some trust purchases.

The banks have tightened the lending criteria for investors, owner occupiers as well as first home buyers. They are requiring borrowers to have more deposit and stronger incomes. They are ensuring these clients don't default and if they do that the banks don't lose!

Investors have been heavily hit by bank changes over the last 7-8 years with APRA telling the major banks that they want their percentage of investment loans to be less and around 35% of their total lending. They realised that this was an impossibility and have slowly changed back and relinquished those requirements.

Borrowing Capacity.

In calculating for borrowing capacity for investors the banks are adding "buffer" for their protection onto interest rates and ensuring much more security (deposit) is required. For the best part of the last 30 years the buffer was 2.5% on top of the standard variable. This was not readily known. Over the last 3-4 years, since Covid, this buffer has risen across the board and is now 3% above the standard variable. On top of that, most banks will also add that 3% onto all existing loans when calculating your borrowing capacity. Remember they are making sure there is minimal risk. For them!

It is much more difficult to get a 95% or 90% loan and even the 80% loan is only given against conservative valuations. This ensures the bank has far more security than ever before. This massively drops the amount one can borrow and massively restricts your ability to duplicate into more assets. Again, the crazy thing is that the holding cost of the new assets is still minimal and well within most people's capacity.

We (LPWA P/L) state to our clients to use a bank that will use a minimum of 80% of the projected rental income when assessing your borrowing capacity. Unfortunately, not all banks will use this figure. Most will not use the full amount you are receiving now with an existing property and some a much smaller percentage on all the existing rental amounts already achieved on other rental properties, which reduces capacity.

So, it's not just a simple scenario of all things are even and all the same for every person.

This is one of the reasons why you must use a licensed Finance Broker who understands all of this and will control it for you.

Have a broker working for YOU!

Have the broker on your team!

It costs you nothing to use a broker and they will have access to far more lending products than the banks alone and have availability for "brokers only" products. Most of these are not available from a retail bank.

Valuations!

Sometimes the logic of things just does not make sense. It seems logical that all banks' valuations would be true and accurate of the "real" price of a property. Unfortunately, this is not the case and to build serious wealth in property, you not only must understand valuations but also be in control of them. This has always been a huge problem and difficulty for investors and today this control is taken even further away from the borrower than ever before.

Why do banks call on valuations?

You would logically think they would do this to find out an accurate assessment of the market value of the property. Unfortunately, this is not the actual case. The banks call on a valuation on a property for security purposes. (***You*** pay for this in most cases but rarely see or receive it).

It is for their purpose, so as they have someone else to legally sue other than yourself if you default.

The banks give instructions indirectly to valuers to value property under the pretence that you will default on the loan and hence they, under a "90-day fire sale" scenario, will be able to sell the property and regain the money lent to you.

Rarely do they ever lose as you have put up security of 10 or 20% minimum deposit. The maximum the medium house price has ever dropped in an Australian capital city is 7% which was in Sydney way back in 1989, after a massive surge in price growth the previous few years.

Again, it is also worth remembering that the drop was predominantly from expensive properties that few can buy anyway. Another reason why we suggest clients stay in the lower quartile of property values.

Real Estate valuation is a "subjective" opinion and certainly not an exact science.

When a bank calls on a valuer to value a property, they also disclose the purchase price before the valuation occurs to the valuer doing the job. The valuer must work out an achievable value on the property if it is sold within a three-month "forced" period on behalf of the bank. They are working out what they believe can be attained under a worst-case scenario!

They also already know what the contract price is which means they have information that will bias their decision.

All valuers carry an indemnity policy usually of at least a couple of million dollars. This is in case the property does have to be sold within this "fire sale 90-day period" and in case the price they value the property at is not met by the sale. If this does occur the bank can sue the valuer for the difference.

So, it is easy to see why the valuer will be conservative and of course why the banks call on valuations. They want as much protection for themselves as possible.

It becomes even more difficult for investors who are purchasing an "off the plan" house and land package in a new development.

Valuers are instructed to use "comparable" sales from within the area, no more than 12 months old.

It is extremely rare that anyone will have resold a property in a new development within that timeframe. So, the valuer must find "other" sales that they "believe" are comparable. If they know the banks want them to be conservative anyway and they need to protect themselves against being sued, then of course they are going to find sales that are comfortable for their decision. Often these sales are out of the area, much older and not in the actual estate being developed.

I have been seeing this happen for over 28 years that I have been in this industry. This exact scenario happened to one of my clients in November 2024. The exact same property was valued by two different companies/valuers on the 11th November 2024 and 27th November 2024. Both valuers were given exactly the same details being the build contract with all plans and specifications. One valuer assessed the property value at $750,000 and the second valuer at $830,000.

Reading the reports is a very interesting exercise. One uses properties from out of the area on sales that were done some time ago using properties that are 8-10 years old. That report is not comparing apples with apples.

The only way we can work out the true market value of a property is to do our own homework.

We must compare what we are buying with **the most recent owner occupier sales**. They must have the same size land, same size house, age and quality which includes the landscaping and all finishes.

The demand we have in Australia for housing blocks is massively strong. Developers sell the land at their designated amount knowing that they will achieve those prices. You don't see developers discounting blocks of land in demand areas to often!

Getting valuers to accept these sales can often be difficult because they are "new" sales and not resales from within the last 12 months. (remember the criteria that they use being sales within the last 12 months).

I have seen hundreds of valuations where the land has been put down as much lower than the actual sale price, even though there maybe another hundred of these blocks recently sold to owner occupiers who are building their family home in the area.

These people are the ones who set the value of the land as they are prepared to pay that price to come and live in the area.

So, from your prospective there are two concerns and inaccuracies with the valuation system.

The first is the bank asks the valuer what the property will sell for "if and when" the client defaults.

This means the valuer may have a negative thought against the valuation when doing the job and will of course be conservative with their opinion.

Secondly, the valuer has a conflict of interest because the instructions he/she has received are in the banks interest and certainly not the purchases.

They will be protecting the bank and of course themselves. In the courts, the law will allow and accept a 15-20% discrepancy. If you were paying $800,000 for a property, the law would accept discrepancy of $120,000 to $160,000.

In my 28+ years of wealth building, I have seen most valuations from registered valuers, valuing properties with major discrepancies. A lot of these have been with my own properties and unfortunately if you are not understanding and controlling the complete finance process, then you are massively restricting your ability to build wealth in the period you require to reach your goals.

Banks have a policy not to disclose the valuation to clients.

Personal Story:

I purchased land in 2001 and had a brand-new home built on it in the suburb of Carina, Brisbane. The whole process was one I would never wish to do again (project manage my own house construction) and took around 18 months to finally complete.

I took possession of the keys at completion the day before Brisbane won it's second of three AFL Premierships. I remember this well as I was able to take my family to the Gabba two days later to see them bring home the cup.

The market in Brisbane throughout 2002 was running hot and at that time, I realised that I had gained significant equity in the property to "go again".

I called on a valuation but gave instructions to the valuation company to not let the valuer set foot onto the premises until I was there. I had done my research on the whole area and had comparable sales data, but more than that, I wanted the valuer to take into account all the add On's that I had put into the property.

I had added an extra garage, concreted totally under the house for a gym and storage space, as it was a traditional Queenslander on poles and had added a pool in the back yard with substantial landscaping.

As I expected the valuer came to the house with his "comparable sales data" which he was not keen to disclose but I forced out of him with direct questions.

The property was worth around $500,000 and he was using sales evidence that "proved" to him it was worth no more than $360,000. His evidence was a run down four-bedroom dump that was seriously falling over and should have been bulldozed three up from my place on a lot of 600m2. What he was not considering was that here was a 100% brand new home (had not depreciated at all) with land size of 830m2.

That was his direct comparison!

So, I had more than a third more land and that old dump sold for $365,000 and was really land value only. The house as stated was a dump and over 60 years old.

Houses in Australia have a 40-year life span and are 100% depreciated at the 40-year mark. In effect they are not worth anything after that age.

I eventually got my valuation and used it to buy another two houses but if left to the young valuer, who incidentally had 14 valuations to complete that day (no wonder he was rushing through mine!) I would have had no equity to use and would not have been able to buy the next two houses which have of course grown in value as well since that time.

Today in 2025 we have an even more difficult valuation situation to "get around".

The financial industry now must use a system named "Valex".

The "Valex" system is one that forces financial institutes when calling for a valuation to submit all applications into this system which literally becomes a lottery. The valuations are designated out to valuer's lottery style.

The valuers have no contact other than the paperwork things are submitted with and proceed to do "their" valuation under the belief that the financier wants a conservative valuation for security purposes.

They know that the banks' policy is not to disclose this valuation they are about to do and that the brokers or employees have been given instructions as such.

We are also in a "new" time where interest rates have been moving upwards and for the first time in decades, we are seeing genuine inflation.

Banks and valuation companies are conservative at the best of times. Today more than ever you must have someone controlling the process for you. You cannot beat the system, but you do need to understand it and how to best work it.

No longer can the financier or broker discuss the valuation or as was in the past, argue a case to prove that higher sales amounts have already been achieved.

The broker can appeal if they have proof and evidence, but it is very unlikely that the valuer will change their opinion.

You must understand that the valuation is a critical tool that you will need and rely on over your wealth building time. It is used by us to show the increase in equity for purposes of duplication.

A valuation is usually just an independent subjective opinion of the value of a property but based on instructions given.

In wealth building, our purpose is to utilize any excess equity to build wealth. The valuation should not be used as a check of purchase price as the person making the assessment may not be comparing exact "apples with apples", as was the case of my Carina property.

There were various policies in respect to valuations with the banks. Some of the major banks had one valuer per postcode or area. Depending upon instructions given, you would struggle to renegotiate increases in equity unless you moved banks. There was very little you could do about it.

It seems unfair but that unfortunately was the way they operated and today it is even worse.

The policy of the banks is to not provide or disclose to a client a copy of "their" valuation.

Try asking your bank for a copy of the valuation on "your" property, which they have security over.

It will be interesting to see how you go. Some have become a little more relaxed but in truth of all the people I have been associated with over the last 28 years, only one in a thousand would have this document and fewer than that have the full valuation and looked it over before moving ahead and going unconditional on finance and hence the purchase.

Remember, "if you are not in control of the valuation, you are not in the ball game".

Therefore, you must use a broker to do the work for you. You need the broker to understand what you require and why.

So, if the banks/ financiers are having similar problems with the new system then how do we as wealth builders get around the situation?

The answer is simple!

You can't get around it if you choose to go with one bank.

We at LPWA P/L are fortunate enough to be able to use different finance brokers.

So, we can "go again" with another lender if one lending group is forced to use a valuation that is in our eyes poor.

What we are sometimes able to do is to do a "check" valuation before the formal valuation is applied for.

This gives us some idea of how things are going to work out before submission and some ammunition to give to a valuer when they contact us for confirmation of details on the property or agents details for them wanting to get into the property.

Even if it is "off the Plan" they still must go to the site before preparing the plan.

There are different types of valuations done on properties.

We need a "full" valuation done each time which means the valuer has to enter the property.

Some banks and financial institutions do "drive by" valuations and work out their value by paperwork. These can be very dangerous as we may not be getting a true reading on the property.

The most important thing for all of us who wish to use the valuation for wealth building is that it is disclosed to us and the information used to be made available. This at least allows you to check that the valuer has taken all the facts into account.

Obviously, the instructions given will determine this. We need the information of the valuation **for future purposes** so as we have an initial benchmark to use. The date the valuation was carried out is critical as future sales after this date can be used to show increase in equity from that time. Again, this is exactly what I was able to do with the Carina property and many others.

Obtaining a valuation on a "new" property in a "new" area brings up further difficulties. Valuers in most cases want "resales" as evidence of the true market value of an area as previously mentioned.

Unfortunately, in new developments, including Master Planned communities, these do not exist.

Often valuers will "find" comparative sales evidence (in their eyes they are comparative) that in truth may not be a real comparison. I've seen "sales evidence" used in valuations on "similar" property sold 10-20kms away in completely different areas. Often these properties are resales that are also 15-20 years old, sometimes older!

They are not comparing apples with apples but happy to use these "comparative sales evidence" as they are around the price that they want the valuation to be at.

As mentioned in the court of law a 20% variation is acceptable from the valuer's perception of market value.

When I am looking at the market value in these types of developments, I look at the only two components that make up it's whole.

The land value and the value (cost) of the improvements.

It's easy to find what the land developer is selling blocks of land for at that time and in that stage release. They will have a price list and be able to show you via contract what has already sold. They don't drop their land prices. As a matter of fact, they increase them steadily with every stage release.

It's also not difficult to find what it costs for construction of a sized building. Most builders are around the same cost pending size of buildings, products used in construction and possible variation on the difference in quality and cost of inclusions.

So, if we understand that the valuer may not have our interests at heart when doing the valuation because they may be under instructions and wish to protect themselves and the finance company, then what can and should we do?

As an independent person doing all this on your own, you need to look at a bank that values at market value and discloses a copy of the valuation to the client. You seriously will struggle to find this on your own.

You will need to use a broker to help you achieve this but be careful there as well and spend some time before hand speaking and ensuring they know exactly what **you** want.

Most brokers will say that they can achieve this for you and know what you are after, but in truth and in the end they may not and only be saying this to get your business.

Simply the valuation needs to be disclosed to you and accepted by the lending institution that is supplying you the finance.

It must include:

- Replacement costs of improvements (in conjunction with the Quantity Surveyors Report)
- Market rent and examples of rentals achieved.

If the valuation does not include all these points, it may not be a true reflection of market value and can cost you valuable equity.

Remember as a person wishing to build wealth and expand your portfolio, you either get a bank to accept these criteria when valuing or find another bank that will.

Again, I repeat myself because of the importance of this regarding your wealth building. The valuation must be disclosed to you for future reference and the criteria above used each and every time.

Non-Cross Collateralisation.

To ensure you have the most flexibility possible for future duplication purposes and future release of equity and security of assets, we strongly suggest you do not cross collateralise your assets.

In short it means tying the security of your assets together with one back. Our structure is to use multiple banks to avoid this. Sometimes we need to connect some assets to enable our best chance of "going again" but for long term wealth building, it is very much in your interests to have a structure where banks have security of just the asset that the loan is designated against.

We do this simply by setting up an independent loan against a property for the deposit and costs associated with purchasing the new asset. We need to be aware that the valuation on the new asset with a separate bank "will most likely" be conservative. That means the separate deposit and costs loan (which is normally interest only) must be sufficient to cover it all.

We at LPWA P/L work with you to ensure we know what the security is each time. You are never borrowing more for the property, but maybe getting a larger percentage of borrowings from one property rather than the other. Knowing the security, you have put into a property allows you the knowledge of what valuation you need on that property to achieve once the property has moved up in value to enable you to access your deposit and costs for the next purchase.

Understanding all of this and having the right structure, gives you without doubt the best opportunity of getting to your end goals.

The Logic of property valuations seems to have no Logic.

Chapter 6

Questions To Know.

How do you build wealth?

It's simple really. You can only build wealth by acquiring assets. You hold the assets and over time the assets increase in value. That is building wealth and having wealth.

Unfortunately, we are educated to think having money is being wealthy. It's not! Money devalues over time.

It is impossible to be wealthy if you don't own assets!

So, to build wealth you need a structure that will allow you over time to "duplicate" your assets without you having to save for deposits every time and without you having to put a lot of "after tax" money into holding these assets.

In other words, use equity for deposits and costs every time and make sure the rent and tax deductions pay for all your holding costs or at least within your budget.

To build wealth you must use "leverage". In real words this means "other" people's money!

So, use money from the banks! To change a car tyre, you need a jack for "leverage". We can't just lift a car; we need the leverage of the jack to help.

It's the same principle if you want to build wealth. **You must use leverage.**

The other secret ingredient you must have to build wealth is **"compound growth".**

Compound growth is "growth on growth".

So, once you have multiple properties you are getting growth on all of these. By understanding the banks rules and regulations we can use "our" equity in our own home or other investments for the use of deposits and the extra costs associated with purchasing investment properties.

If we "use" not "lose" your equity for investment, then the interest is deductable against our tax paid from our main employment!

Done correctly we can get this tax back every pay day or each quarter if we are self-employed. Your accountant should know how to do this by submitting a tax variation form.

That makes a big difference for cash-flow and allows us to hold many properties and of course gain the necessary compound growth required for us to be wealthy.

Financial Independence.

Why? Most people recognise that once they stop working their lifestyle will dramatically change as their superannuation will give them nowhere near what they have now on a weekly basis! So, the why is simple. To ensure they maintain a decent living standard.

Once a target (goal) is set you must choose and use a vehicle.

Time passes quickly, so you're not going to get to your destination meandering along.

You need **a VEHICLE** to drive you to where you want to be.

Our vehicle is **'Real Estate'.**

The banks see 'Real Estate' as the strongest asset class and hence will allow much more **'leverage'** with real estate than anything else.

So, you've set your target and chosen a vehicle.

What ensures the vehicles moves is the **"FUEL"** you put in the tank.

Our fuel is **Income, Tax and Equity.**

The more of each you have and can "use", not "lose", the quicker and more you can achieve. So, combining all of this involves structure.

Your structure is the key to success and security along the way.

Knowledge of the structure includes understanding the correct finance structure, tax deductions and of course the correct asset being "Real Estate."

Once you have the knowledge you must **start** the vehicle and create movement and **ACTION.**

Without **ACTION** you go nowhere and nowhere today actually takes you backwards.

Why? Target? Vehicle? Fuel? Structure? Knowledge? Action?

Do I need to invest?

The answer is nearly every person must invest if they want more than the pension in retirement.

Superannuation is just nowhere near enough for most people and not all have "super". **700 Australians over the age of 65 retire every day. 630 of these register for the old age pension. Today the pension is around $29,754 per year for a single and for a couple it is $44,855**

I think this answers the question as to do you need to invest!

Using Equity/ What is equity?

Equity is simply the money that you own in say your house that is the difference between the debt you owe and the value of your property. Pending how much income you can prove you are earning each year; the banks will allow you to borrow back your equity up to 80% of "their" valuation on your property. If that is sufficient, you can use that "equity" for a deposit and all costs in purchasing another property.

How do I increase my equity?

To have an increase in your equity, you need the value of the property to have increased or the debt to have decreased. You also need a valuer that is accepted by your finance company to recognise the increase.

Decreasing debt on your own home should always be a genuine goal as the money you pay for mortgage on your own home loan has no tax deductions.

In other words, you have already paid tax before you pay your weekly mortgage.

Of course, the easiest way to increase equity is to just wait and let time take its course. Good quality house and land product in capital cities doubles in a cycle which on average is around 7-10 years.

Once you know there is an increase in value of your property, you can call on a valuation from a finance institution and if there is an increase and you have serviceability (income) then you are away again and have ability to purchase again.

How to acquire property?

It may sound like a simple question, but most don't know the basics and how to do this correctly.

First you must understand what type of property to buy and suits your borrowing capacity. We only suggest 100% brand new property off the plan. There are many reasons for this but mainly it is far better tax wise and far less problems with new v old. You also only pay stamp duty on the land and although you pay interest on borrowed funds during the construction period, these are all borrowed and hence tax deductable in most cases in the first year of the property been operational.

So, if you are buying property, the contract **MUST be "subject to finance"!**

The finance broker will need complete counter signed contracts (by you, the land developer and builder) before they can submit to financial institution for finance approval.

If the contracts are signed **"subject to finance"** you are not committed until this full finance has been received!

By having fully approved finance it means you have everything covered from start to property completion and available for tenants.

Accountants and financial planners can advise you on the best structure for you to hold assets.

Of late SMSF's have become a very popular entity that people are using to purchase property using leverage.

The first thing you must do is look at your scenario and work out what you can do. If you are paying tax, then it would be most likely an accountant will say to purchase the property in your own name. You need the tax deductions and hence the purchasing entity needs to be paying tax!

What is your process and first step?
(with LPWA P/L)

Usually, the first step is to attend a meeting with a LPWA representative.

They will take some details from you and arrange a free assessment of your borrowing capacity from our Australian finance broker.

This is vital as until this is clear to you, we are unable to know what you can do.

At the meeting you will discuss what it is you want to achieve and your timeframe to achieve this within.

This is the most important thing you will do and is usually the hardest thing to choose and decide on.

If you are interested to investigate LPWA P/L further after this appointment and follow up with the finance broker, we will show you some examples of properties that are available for you to purchase. With these properties we will give you cash flow examples of exactly what your costs to hold the property will be. If you are comfortable with this, you can request to sign an expression of interest form which secures the property off the market whilst contracts are being drawn up.

Contracts are signed subject to finance approval. The lawyer representing you will explain over the phone and/or via email/Zoom what needs to happen and what is the procedure to settlement of the property.

At LPWA P/L we prefer to have contracts sent to the lawyer representing you prior to you signing.

The lawyer will explain all the protective mechanisms we at LPWA P/L have put into place for your protection.

The lawyer will fully explain what your commitment is to the contract and what the land vendor and builder's commitment is to you. The lawyer will explain when deposits need to be paid and will help in this transaction. The financier will also have all bank accounts and transfers set up for each client to ensure settlement can occur.

Why property?

Property is and will always be the strongest asset class. The banks recognize this and hence why they are prepared to lend and give so much leverage for property compared to any other asset class.

Why should I not do it myself? Why should I use someone or some company to help?

The short answer is that you can do it yourself. Most of our clients choose not to do this because they are professionals in their league and do what they do well.

In turn they let us do what we or others do well.

There is very little chance you could do things at the same costs after taking all things into consideration including your time spent on the job.

There are many other reasons, but the main one is for peace of mind knowing that we know what we are doing and do it very well.

We at LPWA P/L have had many years' experiences in the Australian Investment property industry and can secure the right property in the correct structure for all clients. We ensure that clients are protected legally, and the product is built correctly to Australian building standards.

We are a private organization that understands the requirements of our clients. We understand the Australian market and Australian culture.

What are the most important points to focus on?

1. Location - Schools, Shops, Family area, Secure safe area, Transport, Jobs and Recreation.

2. Timing - ensure the area has room for growth.

3. Tax Deductions - ensure property meets Australian tax regulations.

Without getting all this right you may not see enough growth in time to meet your financial goals.

I'm self-employed, is this viable for me?

Yes. We have and have had hundreds of clients who are self-employed and who are building a strong portfolio. In some cases, it is a benefit.

Advice?

Don't take advice from anyone who hasn't done it themselves! It seems everyone is an expert when it comes to property. Be smart! As a trade's person would you take advice from someone that hasn't done your job before?

Cashflow.

The best way you can "guarantee" cashflow for property investment is to ensure your property and hence rent is in the affordable bracket. 90% of Australian's rent because they can't afford to buy. It makes sense to always keep rents at a level where all renters can afford it and hence rent your property!

Correct Finance Structure.

Banks will want as much security from you as they possibly can get. In most cases they will want the security of your own home if you wish to purchase an investment using your own equity.

This is called **"cross collateralisation"** and it is the one thing we strongly suggest you do not do!

Property v Real Estate.

Know the difference! Real Estate is LAND. Property is what is built on top of the land.

Land is the only part that goes up!

Who is LPWA P/L?

LPWA P/L is a company that trades as Logic Property Wealth Australia. We are a family business, headed by Simon Meehan who has been involved in the property investment industry since 1996.

LPWA P/L exists to be a profitable organisation, to educate and to facilitate ordinary Australians property portfolios, ensuring their financial freedom.

We work with ordinary Australians who without our help will never be able to achieve financial security. We exist to be an authority in the property investment business.

We develop, and secure land based real estate and structure clients correctly in all areas of finance to ensure duplication of assets and long-term success for financial independence and retirement.

What accreditation does LPWA P/L have?

Under ASIC regulations, all our sales staff hold Sales Agents representative's certificates. Simon Meehan as our main presenter holds a full REIV Real Estate License 073198L.

We are not financial planners.
We are not accountants.
We are not lawyers.

Hence, we cannot give you specific advice regarding these areas of expertise.

We can give you generic examples and talk about what our clients have already done. This is a great way for you to investigate what you can set up and do for yourself.

We do have independent financial planners, accountants, finance brokers and lawyers who work independently under our umbrella.

We have independent property management agents located all over the country that care for our client's assets and find appropriate tenants.

We recommend these companies because we trust them and know that they are highly qualified creditable organisations that understand what we are trying to achieve for our clients.

Why invest in Australian property?

Australian property has been an outstanding long-term investment and is predicted to continue to be a strong secure investment option. Australia continues to have the largest percentage population growth in the world. This along with our natural birth rate ensures strong demand for our residential property for many years to come.

By 2050 Australia's population is predicted to grow by another 20,000,000. That will take us to a total population somewhere near 50,000,000.

For the last 40 years we have averaged around 45,000 blocks nationally that we have developed.

With around 3 people per household, we would need around 7-8 million new residences or 325,000 new residences every year.

We have no chance of producing these numbers and hence demand for property/real estate will continue and potentially an even greater rate than we have ever seen.

What about a purchase in a SMSF?

Purchasing property inside a SMSF has become a very popular thing over the last 10-12 years. (Please see the chapter on SMSF purchasing).LPWA P/L has helped dozens of our clients purchase within a SMSF structure. Very few people can purchase a new house and land product in a SMSF structure as to do this the purchase must be a one contract and very few builders will fund the construction stages.

Today the demand for off the plan property is so strong that builders insist clients fund the construction. LPWA P/L have access to one contract stock because of our length of time in the business and close relationships with land vendors and builders.

We have independent lawyers, financial planners, accountants and finance brokers that can put the required structures in place that completely meet all ASIC requirements.

The benefits of purchasing a property inside a SMSF set up are extensive and very much worth investigating. Most clients use our service to coordinate the whole process. They recognise the risk involved with standard super being invested in managed funds. On average the markets have a severe crash every 7-10 years. They also recognise the high costs associated in yearly fees. Once they have projections shown by independent financial advisors, re the growth of doing this versus keeping Super in managed funds they are quick to recognise the benefits and move in getting LPWA P/L to help put the property acquisition into action.

What growth could we expect in 10 years?

History tells us that the medium home price in Australia doubles in value every 7-10 years and has done so for many decades. We need to recognise this is the medium "house" price and not unit price.

All we are aiming for is the average growth that this country has shown for over 100 years. If we just aim for this type of growth with affordable property, then rents will be assured, and our goals will be met without serious risk. So, if we require the "average" we need to understand what the "average" suburb is like. (please see chapter re Criteria). If we stick to a Capital City with above a million in population and to house and land product, then we give ourselves a genuine chance of obtaining the average growth that the country will achieve in the next 10 years!

Your Capacity.

Everyone will have a different capacity of what they can do. Whether you are buying for living purposes or strictly for investment, the banks will need to know you have capacity to service the loan. They will consider future projected rental income, but they will also look at your income at present to ensure you have capacity to meet the loan repayments. They also need to see that you have a deposit available that can be used for the purchase of the property. Your financier will explain exactly what will be required to purchase the property.

Should I go for a P&I or I/O loan?

All interest associated with the investment property is tax deductable.

An interest only facility gives you a lower monthly payment as no Principal part is attached to this.

The principal part being repaid is **NOT** tax deductable and hence why most investors will go for an **Interest Only** loan.

Recently banks were told by the governing body (APRA) to lower their percentage of investment debt against owner occupier debt to around 35%. APRA have since come out and put a holt to this request. What did happen was that many banks introduced lower owner occupier rates and higher I/O rates. This happened for the first time in my 35 years of borrowing and created an unusual circumstance. From that accountants acquired software that could comfortably divide the P&I from I/O and these low interest loans became popular with investors as well.

Remember if you pay off **"Principal"** you can't reborrow that amount and then claim again the interest component unless it is being used for another deposit and costs of a secondary investment.

How long will it take me to see the results from my investment?

This depends on market conditions. In a growth market you can see results even before the house is completed and we've had examples of that. In a slow market, it can take two, three or more years before you see enough growth to enable you to see equity gain and duplicate. This depends of course on your loan value ratio and other particular circumstances.

We like clients to focus on property that will at least allow them to duplicate within a 3-4- year maximum period. Obviously, this cannot be guaranteed but looking at the property cycle and the basics of demand for property, it will give you a good chance of obtaining this goal.

How long does it take for me to have enough equity to purchase another property?

This depends on your finance structure, loan value ratio, the state of the market at the time and other particular circumstances. You should work this through yourself by staying on top of growth and finance options, however, most don't and hence need companies like ours to help them ascertain if they can buy again.

How do I know when I'm ready to duplicate?

This is something you need to work at. It will mean not only monitoring the growth of your property, which you can do through property sites like RP Data, but also revising and reviewing your borrowing capacity and working to reduce any principle that you have on debt which is locked in on non-growth assets or even your principal place of residence.

What sort of return should we expect per annum?

Returns will fluctuate from year to year, but the average medium home over a ten-year period is higher than

7% and depending on the area it could be as high as 9%-10% or more.

We have seen some years where property values have jumped by more than 30%.

We have also seen times when the market has been slow, and little growth has occurred over 5-6 years. If you are serious about Australian property you should invest with the idea of never selling.

How do I know I am paying the right price?

You should use comparable sales that owner-occupiers have paid in the area to ensure you are paying market price. It is not difficult to obtain land sales evidence. We also know accurately what it costs to construct and the difference in price of a fully completed package.

Construction prices can vary on size and quality but in general if you shop around, you can ascertain what a fair price for construction will be.

Is a deposit for holding a property required?

Yes! With most groups you are required to sign an expression of interest which involves a $1000 fully refundable amount. This expression of interest allows you time to then have all your documentation done in conjunction with solicitor acting for you.

This gives both you and the solicitor time to go over the contract and ensure everything is in place and understood. In some cases, the land vendor will require a 10% deposit to be paid when signing documentation before they will counter sign the contract.

You will need this contract counter signed before any finance company will approve your loan. What this means is that your "Property Finance" person will have had to do quite a bit of work for you on your behalf before you purchase a property.

In most cases they will have already set up a line of credit against an asset of yours to ensure you have the necessary funds available to pay the necessary deposit and required monies for settlement of land. The lawyer will also explain to you exactly what amount is required at land settlement.

How many properties should I purchase?

Whatever is appropriate for you to meet your goals, and you can afford.

If you are a 1st time investor, we suggest you go slowly to ensure you understand the buying procedure firsthand. This can differ pending your personal circumstances and necessity.

Once you understand how safe and secure your investment is, you should be confident to purchase and maximise your capabilities. This gives you the maximum benefit of compound growth within your structure.

Can my own solicitor here do all my legal work?

If you are buying in the State where you live, the answer is yes.

If it's a solicitor registered in a State other than where you purchase and isn't currently registered in the state where you are purchasing, they will need to organize a solicitor, or we can recommend a panel of solicitors who have acted on behalf of other clients. Some solicitors are registered in multiple states.

How much cash do I need behind me?

If you've got equity in your own home, you do not need any cash, and we suggest you put any cash you have into paying off your own home.

This is because the money you pay on your own home mortgage is not deductable and that debt affects your ability to borrow. If you don't have your own home, you will need around 15% minimum of the purchase price to cover deposit, costs and incidentals.

Can you purchase if you don't own your own property?

Yes. For some people they see it better to never own their own home. Some people prefer to focus on building wealth before they commit to purchasing their own home where the debt is non-deductable.

Should we invest mainly to duplicate?

Duplication is the process that allows you to achieve compound growth.

Without compound growth, it is impossible for you to achieve serious wealth.

Investing is different from picking a place to live in or a place that is chosen for personal purposes like education.

Invest with your brain. Buy to live with using your heart. Always keep both separate.

What is average land content in properties?

Properties all over the country will differ in land content. A new apartment will on average have only 5-10% of its value being the land content. Older properties tend to have a higher land content as the building has depreciated. We ensure that all LPWA properties have a minimum of 30% land value.

When do I sell my houses?

We suggest that you don't sell once you've built a critical mass of property that is compounding. You literally just must sit and forget while your net worth increases by a compounded amount.

Ask your consultant for more info re this matter as it is vital for you to understand in the future for you to have access to your wealth. The only reason you should ever sell is if you must or for another reason that is of benefit to you. Some sell to pay off non deductible debt like their home mortgage and then immediately re borrow much more for new property. They can usually borrow much more as they have minimal or lower non-deductible debt on their own home, hence borrowing capacity is much higher.

What are my risks?

The main risk is cash flow. Cash flow is affected by two things: one is interest rates, which can be combated by locking in your rate. The other is your tenants rent where risk can be reduced using careful planning and insurance options. The rental risk is minimized by location criteria and by keeping prices of property in the lower quartile. This ensures rents are always affordable.

The risk of tenants can be insured. The vacancy rate of house and land product in Capital Cities in Australia now is the lowest it has ever been, and rents will continue to have serious demand as population increases.

What happens if interest rates go up?

We prefer that you investigate locking in your loans as interest rates can affect your cash flow if they rise. This is a personal decision you make however we do know from experience rents increase when rates go up.

If interest rates rise does my rent, go up?

Generally, that's been the experience, however this can take 6-9 months to filter through. Rising interest rates will mean higher inflation and higher inflation will mean the economy is moving and the experience has been that rents increase, and property values also increase.

What is "Fair Market Value?"

The best way to find the Market Value of a property is to compare recent sales in the area that have sold to people who have chosen to live in the area themselves. (Owner Occupiers).

What amount do I borrow?

That depends on you, but it will be between 80%-110% of the purchase price of the investment property.

Will Property Finance brokers get me the best rate?

It will be very close but not necessarily the best rate as the best rate may compromise your ability to duplicate or require greater security than is necessary.

We believe it is better in some circumstances to pay slightly above the best rate but still measure it against the variable rate and have a structure to duplicate to ensure you meet all requirements to give you the absolute best chance of meeting your long-term finance goals. **Please remember interest on investment properties are fully tax deductible and hence interest rates are not quite as important as with your own home loan where you get no deductions.**

What gauge do Property Finance brokers use to calculate borrowing capacity?

This varies from lender to lender as they each have stipulations on income and cost allowances for dependants and other items that you may have under finance. All Australian banks insist that investors must have strong deposit funds plus costs to purchase. This percentage is off the contract price. Banks usually add on 2.5 – 3% on top of the standard variable rate at the time when calculating how much you can borrow. They will usually only use 30% of your gross income as the amount that can be used for all mortgage repayments.

What is LVR?

LVR is Loan Value Ratio and it's the amount the bank will loan you compared to the value of the property. Some people also see LVR as a percentage of your value of asset vs the debt over that asset or your combined LVR being all your value as a % against your total debt.

What is DSR?

DSR is Debt Service Ratio and it's the percentage of the income you generate that a bank will let you allocate to your debt. (The Serviceability)

What is serviceability?

This is simply your cash flow that you generate to service your loan.

Whose names are the titles in and who keeps the deeds?

The titles are in your name or another entity's name that you may choose if need be. The deeds are kept by your bank who is the mortgagee.

What is the best structure to buy an investment property in?

This will depend on where your income comes from but generally in your own name or wherever else you generate income. If you have a complicated structure for generating income, it may be worth referring to your accountant. Finance advisors are worthwhile discussing this with as they can give advice on the benefit of purchasing in trusts and other entities.

Can I top up my equity when I want?

Yes, you can, pending on whether you have taken a fixed loan, interest only loan or principal and interest.

Is an equity loan or a redraw facility better?

It is advisable to always obtain a separate equity loan when raising a deposit for an investment property purchase. Redraw facilities should only be used on your own home for personal expenditure and not for investment.

At tax time it makes life much easier for your accountant to decipher what is personal and what is for investment if you get a separate equity loan each time.

Can you please explain interest during construction?

Interest during construction is simply based on the fact that you have settled the land and therefore you will be paying interest on your land whilst your house is being constructed.

Further, you will be paying progress claims throughout the construction period, which will also attract interest on the outstanding loan as it is drawn down.

Your finance brokers will calculate the amount of interest on the land and construction finance and provide to you the estimate of total outlays that you will need for your acquisition.

"Interest through construction" is deductable.

In most cases the interest through construction will be included in the deposit amount of 30% plus costs that you borrow from equity.

It is worth noting that although we pay money on borrowed amounts through construction, we are saving significant amounts on stamp duty as we are buying "off the plan" and hence only paying stamp duty on the land component and not the total property value.

This is not the case with apartments as we must pay interest on the total purchase price.

When is stamp duty calculated and when do I pay it?

Stamp duty is calculated on the purchase price of your block of land or completed product and it is payable at settlement.

Is all land registered?

Not all land is registered but it must be before you can purchase and settle it. New estates often have a lengthy timeframe before buyers can settle their land as it takes time for council to do what they need to do to have it registered. If you are buying new property, most must contract on land and must wait until the council register the title of the land before settlement can occur.

What if the builder goes broke or can't finish the house?

If the builder fails to comply with its contractual obligation under the building contract, clients have one main form of recourse.

Like all consumers, clients have recourse to the Statutory Insurance Fund, established by the Building Services Authority. This is why it is important we use reliable registered builders.

All states have different laws protecting buyers. Some are more protective than others.

Who is the contract to build with?

The contract is with the builder.

Can I alter the fittings etc of the house?

The short answer is that you can; however, we discourage it because it will cost money in variations.

Out of the thousands of houses we have been involved with construction for our clients, very few have had any alterations.

The houses are designed with a particular specification in mind for immediate tenancy therefore all finishes specified are being done so with tenants in mind.

To what extent should I monitor my building phases?

It is good for you to work closely with your builder during the construction process. You should receive weekly updates on the progress of the property. The builder will monitor the progress, and you can query the builder if there are any noticeable delays or issues apparent.

We suggest you send in an independent building surveyor to do defects report before final payment is made.

This document can be on forward to the builder for immediate rectification. The builder by law must complete all defects for a 6–12–month period, pending which state of Australia you buy in. Your property management agent should also check that all these minor defects are completed before taking the keys and allowing entry to tenants.

Getting this independent building inspection should happen prior to final payment occurring.

What is 'turnkey' and what does it mean to my finished house?

This essentially means that when your house is completed, it's ready for a tenant to move into. All the tenant needs to bring in is his or her own furniture.

How do I pick what estates and property I should purchase?

We naturally research estates that meet all our criteria. We monitor Australian real estate figures, Australian bureau of Statistic figures and are continually looking where government infrastructure spends are happening and projected to happen. We monitor growth rates of different areas around Australia and can see where areas have significant potential for growth.

Why would I buy in Queensland, Perth or Melbourne rather than my own state or area that I personally know?

Quite simply consider where there is potential for further price growth. Migration to a state is very important and when you compare the average home repayment to the average wage, if there is still room for growth then investigate further.

We base our opinion on years of property cycle facts. We look for properties with enough room for growth, so as clients can duplicate from their purchase within a 3–4-year period.

How do I get information on the market?

The Real Estate Institute of Australia (REIA) provides a good breakdown of market information and their relevant associate offices in each state can provide more specific information to the general performance of the capital cities.

We are continually monitoring the markets and are happy to provide you with this information.

Where do you get your information from, i.e. how do you know where the best places for growth are?

We have years of experience in the property industry. Statistically we can work out affordability of an area by looking at mortgage payments V household incomes. This calculation is used specifically by banks when working out borrowing capacity.

Chapter 7

The three most important Questions to ask?

Video link to answer this question: https://youtu.be/EABsi_VkmmQ

The three questions to know or you should know when buying every investment property are;

1. Am I paying the right price?

We have discussed the fact that bank valuations are for the banks security purposes and can vary pending what criteria is used to do the valuation. I have seen many valuations vary significantly from one valuer to another. We must understand that these are carried out for the bank's purposes and for finance reasons.

In truth, the best way to understand if you are paying the right price is to do some homework and find out what both components (land and improvements) are of the package price.

Land can be found by what an agent is selling the most recent blocks for to local owner occupiers. They set the price in an area as they are the ones that are prepared to pay that amount to come live there.

If it is an existing property, then you need to find out what a square metre of land is worth in that area. Using the council rates notice will give you an ideal although these tend to be quite conservative as they are using the UCV (Unimproved capital value) for the land.

With an existing property it is best to look at comparable sales but ensure you are comparing apples with apples!

If it is a new dwelling to be built, it is not difficult to compare builder's prices but again you must compare same size, fittings and dimensions. Things like roof heights and floorings can make a difference and ensure it is a fully 100% turnkey product with landscaping and fencing included.

2. Will it go up in value?

Can I see the potential for growth in the current property cycle? Is there a strong demand in the area?

Is there strong migration happening in the area?

Are there job prospects and infrastructure development happening?

What is the land component of my investment and is it above 30% of the total contract price?

3. Can I rent it continuously and forever?

Is the vacancy rate below 3% in the area?

What is the average household income of the suburb?

Is the rent I am asking affordable for all people in the area?

Is there population growth happening and likely to happen in future? Is my property desirable for everyone that rents?

Chapter 8

Video Links

https://youtu.be/TlVlvJ32Dz8

Get Educated and understand how Australian's retire.

https://youtu.be/EABsi_VkmmQ

Three Questions to Know.

https://youtu.be/atKHnQx8o88

"Welcome to" is simply as it states and explains to viewers who LPWA P/L. is.

https://youtu.be/nf3PNMIwizM

Information to Start.

https://youtu.be/dwSugcF0KA4

Paying off Your Own Home

https://youtu.be/Fh62ZMj2CFE

Building a Property Portfolio

https://youtu.be/o9n6lxf9okc

Inspection Tours

https://youtu.be/m_S36oCP3lw

Self-Managed Super Funds

I was introduced to Simon and LPWA P/L through a work colleague. I was sceptical at first, risk averse and not wanting to do anything that would potentially put us or our retirement savings at risk.

After meeting with Simon, investigating the structure suggested, we took an initial leap with a SMSF property. That was a fantastic decision.

We now have five properties with a secure plan for our retirement, continuing to grow. Since then, we have increased our wealth by over $1 million with minimal outlay.

Finding land, securing finance and building is something I would not have considered doing myself, without the right expertise and guidance. The process has been easy and seamless.

One of the many highlights of this venture has been meeting Simon, he's a bit of a character, but more importantly it's about trust, honesty, integrity and knowing he has our best interests at heart!

We highly recommend you investigate LPWA P/L for your own future benefits.

Simon Meehan | Trust | Integrity | Honesty | Peace of mind | Happy Retirement

Regards, Aylene Baldwin

"Inspired by my father's success with Logic, we invested just three years ago, and were recently able to purchase our second investment poperty. Thanks to the knowledge passed on by Simon, my wife and I have never been more confident about our financial future."

Shannon Vass, Icon Constructions.

"LPWA have enabled my wife and I to apply their basic structures and disciplines to effectively duplicate our property portfolio. We had been reasonably active property investors for almost 10 years before I met Simon, however we did have some flaws on our initial approach.

We had got to a point where we could no longer increase our portfolio due to our unstructured approach to property investing. Simon and the team at Logic helped us understand and apply some basic but highly important principals to maximise our income and investing stream. We have recommended many friends to Simon and will continue to use LPWA as we continue to expand our portfolio."

James & Louisa Zocchi

We can't thank Simon and his team enough for what he's helped us achieve. When we first started, we had zero properties and at our age, late 40's and early 50's, and in our circumstances, we honestly didn't think entering the property market was even possible.

Simon showed us what was achievable with the right guidance and support. We now, just 12 months later, are holding over $3 million worth of real estate. His knowledge of the property market and clear guidance made all the difference.

Simon and his team didn't just help us buy properties; he helped us build a future.

His genuine care, transparency, and attention to detail gave us total confidence every step of the way. We're incredibly grateful for his support and wouldn't hesitate to recommend Logic Property Wealth Australia and Logic Finance to family and friends. Everyone needs to invest to have a decent retirement but unfortunately most don't do anything as they believe financially, they cannot afford it. Our full investment portfolio costs us after tax no money to hold. Investigate for yourself what you can potentially do. We can guarantee it will be worthwhile.

Ben and Angela Kay, Nambour Qld.

"As someone who has invested in property previously, Simon and his team have certainly made the process simple with demonstrable benefits illustrating why property is the way to long term wealth building.

Simon has been great to work with. No question or request has gone unanswered. We are looking forward to building a long term relationship with Simon and as he says, this is not a get rich quick scheme but rather a get wealthy slowly plan delivering long term security through sensible and logical long term planning. The longest journey begins with the smallest steps - thanks Simon"

Jason & Ange Currey

"After what felt like an endless search through dozens of property investment seminars, filled with confusing jargon and unrealistic promises, I was absolutely thrilled to finally discover a company that spoke my language. I went home and told my wife "I have found the group to work with". Simon Meehan presented straightforward, easy-to-understand information about how to invest your hard-earned money into property, without any of the usual "crap". I instantly felt a sense of comfort and trust that had been missing for so long. That pivotal moment with LPWA P/L was 16 years ago, and to this day, I remain a satisfied client and friend of "Logic Property". We have made significant gain in our portfolio to the point where we are financially independent and set up for a quality retirement.

David M.

I cannot thank Simon and the team at Logic Property enough! As a financial manager in the Build industry, I thought I had a good handle on numbers, but when it came to structuring our personal finances and self-managed super fund, my wife and I were completely out of our depth. Simon is an absolute legend and guided us every step of the way and got us to a financial position we never would have dreamed of. The process was seamless, and his expertise and patience made all the difference. Now, we are structured correctly, set up for the future, and have total confidence in our financial direction.

If you're looking for someone who genuinely cares and knows their stuff, I couldn't recommend Simon highly enough!

Nic Fletcher, Contracts Manager

Hi Team,

Thanks so very much for your prompt and efficient work, follow through and feedback with this whole process; it's been a pleasure and delight working with you and the team.

Just to clarify one of Si's comments; we've appreciated and liked working with you from the outset and that "like" has only increased as we've progressed; it's particularly pleasing to work with quality professionals who are people of their word and do what they say they will do, or at least give it their best shot with prompt communication concerning updates/ progress; thank you and very much appreciated.

Also, thanks Si & Glenn; you both rock (paper & scissors), continue to be superstars and are gratefully appreciated.

Cheers, David & Janelle

Please scan for my contact details or to request an appointment to ask questions re "The Logic of Property".